ANIMALS OF THE GRASSLANDS

Kangaroos

by Kaitlyn Duling

BLASTOFF!
2
READERS

BELLWETHER MEDIA · MINNEAPOLIS, MN

Blastoff! Readers are carefully developed by literacy experts to build reading stamina and move students toward fluency by combining standards-based content with developmentally appropriate text.

Level 1 provides the most support through repetition of high-frequency words, light text, predictable sentence patterns, and strong visual support.

Level 2 offers early readers a bit more challenge through varied sentences, increased text load, and text-supportive special features.

Level 3 advances early-fluent readers toward fluency through increased text load, less reliance on photos, advancing concepts, longer sentences, and more complex special features.

★ **Blastoff! Universe**

Reading Level

Grades
1–3

Grade
4

Grade
K

This edition first published in 2021 by Bellwether Media, Inc.

No part of this publication may be reproduced in whole or in part without written permission of the publisher. For information regarding permission, write to Bellwether Media, Inc., Attention: Permissions Department, 6012 Blue Circle Drive, Minnetonka, MN 55343.

Library of Congress Cataloging-in-Publication Data

Names: Duling, Kaitlyn, author.
Title: Kangaroos / by Kaitlyn Duling.
Description: Minneapolis, MN : Bellwether Media, Inc., 2021. | Series: Blastoff! readers: animals of the grasslands | Includes bibliographical references and index. | Audience: Ages 5-8 | Audience: Grades K-1 | Summary: "Relevant images match informative text in this introduction to kangaroos. Intended for students in kindergarten through third grade"--Provided by publisher.
Identifiers: LCCN 2019054187 (print) | LCCN 2019054188 (ebook) | ISBN 9781644872277 (library binding) | ISBN 9781618919854 (ebook)
Subjects: LCSH: Kangaroos--Juvenile literature.
Classification: LCC QL737.M35 D85 2021 (print) | LCC QL737.M35 (ebook) | DDC 599.2/22--dc23
LC record available at https://lccn.loc.gov/2019054187
LC ebook record available at https://lccn.loc.gov/2019054188

Editor: Christina Leaf   Designer: Laura Sowers

Printed in the United States of America, North Mankato, MN.

Table of Contents

Life in the Grasslands

red kangaroo

Several kinds of kangaroos live across Australia. Many of these **marsupials** roam the flat grasslands.

This wide-open **biome** is hot and dry.

Red Kangaroo Range

range = ☐

N
W ✦ E
S

Kangaroos can quickly
cover long distances
on the grasslands.

They have big feet
and powerful legs.
They use these to hop
across the open land.

When kangaroos hop, they reuse **energy**. The power from landing pushes them back up.

Special Adaptations

powerful legs

big feet

This saves energy so they can hop farther and longer.

Handling the Heat

Kangaroos have **adapted** to their hot biome. They are active during the cool evenings.

They rest in the shade
during the day.

Kangaroos **pant** in the heat.

When it is very hot,
they lick their forearms.
These wet spots move
heat away from their
bodies when they dry.

Food and water can be **scarce** on the grasslands.

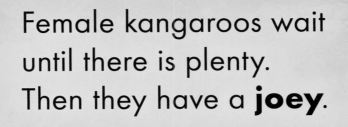

Female kangaroos wait until there is plenty. Then they have a **joey**.

joey

Finding Food

Kangaroos are **herbivores**. They eat tough grasses and leafy plants.

Over time, their teeth wear down and fall out. New ones move in to take their place.

Kangaroo Diet

kangaroo
grass

bottle
washers

black bluebush

The grasslands are dry. Kangaroos can survive on very little water.

The plants they eat keep them **hydrated**. Their **kidneys** hold extra water, too.

Red Kangaroo Stats

Least Concern	Near Threatened	Vulnerable	Endangered	Critically Endangered	Extinct in the Wild	Extinct

conservation status: least concern

life span: up to 23 years

On the driest days,
kangaroos dig for water
in dried-up creeks.

The hot grasslands are
no match for kangaroos.
Happy hopping!

Glossary

adapted—changed over a long period of time

biome—a large area with certain plants, animals, and weather

energy—the power to move and do things

herbivores—animals that only eat plants

hydrated—having a healthy amount of water

joey—a baby kangaroo

kidneys—organs that remove waste products from the blood and produce pee

marsupials—mammals that carry their young in a pouch on the stomach

pant—to breathe with short, quick breaths

scarce—in short supply

To Learn More

AT THE LIBRARY

Kenney, Karen Latchana. *Kangaroo Mobs.* Minneapolis, Minn.: Jump!, 2020.

Owings, Lisa. *From Joey to Kangaroo.* Minneapolis, Minn.: Lerner Publishing Group, 2017.

Parkes, Ella. *Let's Explore Australia.* Minneapolis, Minn.: Lerner Publishing Group, 2018.

ON THE WEB

FACTSURFER

Factsurfer.com gives you a safe, fun way to find more information.

1. Go to www.factsurfer.com.

2. Enter "kangaroos" into the search box and click Q.

3. Select your book cover to see a list of related content.

Index

The images in this book are reproduced through the courtesy of: Bradley Blackburn, front cover; Brad Leue/ Alamy, pp. 4-5; Michal Pesata, pp. 6-7; Jason Benz Bennee, p. 7; olaser, p. 8; Simon McLoughlin, p. 9; Cindy Hopkins/ Alamy, pp. 10-11; Susan Flashman, p. 11; Stephen James Burke, pp. 12-13; Pascale Gueret, p. 13; tructuresxx, pp. 14-15; K.A. Willis, p. 15; Lea Scaddan, pp. 16-17; Young Swee Ming, p. 17 (kangaroo grass); Wikimedia Commons, p. 17 (bottle washer); Mark Marathon/ Wikimedia Commons, p. 17 (black bluebush); Luke Shelley, p. 18; dmvphotos, pp. 18-19; Auscape International Pty Ltd/ Alamy, pp. 20-21; kyslynskahal, p. 21; John Carnemolla, p. 22.